GRIDIRON HEROES

SIX HEISMAN TROPHY® WINNERS

RICHARD J. BRENNER

EAST END PUBLISHING, LTD.

MILLER PLACE, NEW YORK

This book is dedicated to the children of the world and to all of the people who are working, with courage and compassion, to make planet Earth greener, safer and more peaceful.

With great appreciation to Phil Schaap at WKCR-FM in New York, for keeping the music alive, and to Louis 'Satchmo' Armstrong, whose swinging playing kept me moving down the home stretch.

My sincere thanks go to Ed Masessa, Janet Speakman, and Alan Boyko of Scholastic Book Fairs, for their continued support. I also want to thank some of the people who assisted my efforts, including Sarah Becker, Temeka Muse, Elliot Markham, and my copy editor, John Douglas.

Photo Credits: Lexington Herald-Leader/Zuma Press and Icon/SMI supplied the cover image of Mark Ingram and the one on P. 3. **Icon/SMI** also supplied the images listed below, with the photographer's name in bold: The cover image of Sam Bradford and the one on P. 9 and P. 10 **J.P Wilson**; P. 12 **June Frantz-Hunt**; the cover image of Tim Tebow and the one on P. 13 **Sports Palm Beach Post/Zuma Press**; P. 14 **Rhona Wise**; P. 17 **Samuel Lewis**; P. 19 **Gary Rothstein**; P. 20 **Robert E. Hudson, Jr.**; P. 22 **Kellen Micah**; P. 23 **Craig Ambrosio**; P. 24 **Kevin Reece**; P. 26 **John Sommers**; The remaining photographs were supplied by Getty Images, as per the following: P. 4 **Kevin C. Cox**; P. 6 **Dave Martin**; P. 27 **Mathew Stockman**; P. 28 **Tom Hauck**; P. 31 **Ronald C. Modra**.

ISBN: 0-943403-78-2 * 978-0-943403-78-6

This book was not authorized by the Heisman Trophy Trust® or by any of the players or teams mentioned in this book.

Published by EAST END PUBLISHING, LTD.
18 Harbor Beach Road
Miller Place, NY 11764

Printed in the United States of America by Universal Printing Co.

Richard J. Brenner, America's best-selling sportswriter, has written more than 80 exciting sports titles. For details on how to order some of the available titles, see the last page of this book or send an email to: rjbrenner1@gmail.com.

Mr. Brenner is also available to speak at schools and other venues. For details, including fees, you may e-mail him directly at: rjbrenner1@gmail.com, or write to him c/o EEP, 18 Harbor Beach Road, Miller Place, NY 11764.

AUTHOR'S MESSAGE: For many years, Native American groups have been appealing to sports teams not to use names and logos that many people find offensive. Out of respect for, and in support of those appeals, I have chosen not to use such names in this book.

MARK INGRAM
2009 HEISMAN TROPHY WINNER

MARK INGRAM

When Mark Ingram, Junior enro[lled] at the University of Alabama [in] 2008, he became a proud mem[ber] of a football program that had produ[ced] a history of spectacular success on [the] gridiron. The Crimson Tide had won [23] Southeastern Conference championsh[ips] and 12 national titles. 'Bama had also s[ent] a long line of All-American alumni to [the] NFL, including Pro Bowl runni[ng] backs Shaun Alexander and Bo[bby] Humphrey and Super-Bowl-winni[ng] quarterbacks Bart Starr, Joe Nama[th,] and Kenny Stabler. The one promin[ent] item missing from their Hall [of] Champions display was a Heism[an] Trophy, the most prestigious indivi[dual] award in college football.

When 'Bama head coach Nick Sa[ban] offered the football scholarship to Ingr[am,] he didn't even guarantee the running ba[ck a] starting role, let alone discuss the possib[ility] of winning awards. But Ingram had c[ome] a long way from the day when, as an eig[ht-] year-old, he'd started running toward [the] wrong end zone, before he finally tur[ned] around and scored his first-ever touchdo[wn.]

"We were yelling, 'Mark, the o[ther] way,'" recalled his mother Shor[ra,] who is a social worker. "'Turn aro[und] and run the other way.'"

Ingram's ability quickly caught [the] eye of Joe Delaney, the head foot[ball] coach at Michigan's Grand Blanc H[igh] School.

"Physically, he had something [that] most other kids don't have, but he also [had] an unusual amount of maturity and po[ise,]" said Delaney, who made the decision to [...]

Ingram as a ninth grader, only the third time in his 17 years of coaching at Grand Blanc that he has chosen to start a freshman.

"I wasn't going to just throw him out on the field if he wasn't ready to handle the pressure, socially and academically, as well as athletically. I wanted to make sure that he would succeed in the classroom and also be accepted by his teammates."

"I called his grandfather, who assured me that Mark made friends quite easily and that when it came to schoolwork, I shouldn't worry, either. 'Coach, you don't have to be concerned,' his grandfather told me. 'If he gets even a C in any of his classes, he won't be playing football.'"

Ingram easily fulfilled his grandfather's promises, earning B's and better in the

him fielding punts, returning kicks, and playing as a defensive back. I just didn't want to take him off the field."

Unfortunately for Delaney, Ingram decided to switch to Southwest Academy in Flint, Michigan for his senior year, because the Trojans' coach employed a pro-style, I-formation offense, while Delaney was planning to use a spread formation. Ingram fit right into his new school and set a torrid pace on the gridiron, where he rushed for more than 1,700 yards and 24 touchdowns. When Ingram, who won All-State honors, was asked for a self-assessment, he expressed confidence in his abilities, without coming off as boastful or unaware of areas of his game that needed upgrading.

"I have a good combination of power and

Ingram set Flint city single-game records with 377 rushing yards and seven touchdowns in his senior season at Southwest Academy.

classroom and winning over his teammates with his play, his personality, and his priorities.

"The first thing he did after someone complimented his rushing was to praise the offensive line," said Delaney. "He's a very humble, team-first person. A fantastic kid."

In his freshman season, Ingram led the Bobcats to a league and district championship, the first in the school's history, and in his junior year he averaged more than seven yards-per-carry, while being on the field for nearly every play of the season.

"When he got by the line and into the secondary, he would just run over people," said Delaney. "It was a mismatch. But I also had

speed," said Ingram. "I can get the tough yards, but can also make a move and break a big run. I run good routes and catch the ball well. I'm versatile. I want to improve my pass blocking and have a better awareness of the blitz."

Ingram owes his athletic ability to a fortunate gene pool: Both his maternal grandfather, Art Johnson, and his father, Mark Ingram, Sr., were football players at Michigan State. Johnson, a defensive back, went on to play in the Canadian Football League, while Ingram, who was an All-American wide receiver for the Spartans, had a 10-year career in the NFL and was the New York

Giants' top receiver when they won Super Bo...
XXV.

But *Little Mark*, as he is known in the fami... owes his success to his work ethic as much ... he does to his genetic inheritance, and th... combination of talent and dedication has wo... the respect and admiration of his grandfather.

"He is better than I ever was," said Johnso... "And *Little Mark* is better than *Big Mark* ev... was, although his dad may not admit it."

Sadly, Ingram's father is currently in jail, b... the two of them remain bonded, the ties ... family and affection strong and unbroke...

"He taught me how to play an... challenged me to constantly improve... recalled Ingram, who speaks to his fath... a few times a week.

"He never just let me win in anythin... he made me earn it. Everything he did for ... helped me develop into the man I am today an... the competitor that I am, on and off the field...

During his freshman season at Alabama, ... 2008, Ingram gained valuable experience at t... collegiate level playing behind the junior runni... back Glen Coffee. Ingram also made significa... contributions to the Crimson Tide's offens... gaining 728 yards rushing and scoring a tea... leading 12 touchdowns, while helping 'Ba... finish with a 12-2 record and the No. 6 ranki... in two major polls. That bright beginning did ... assure that Ingram would be named the start... for the 2009 season, even after Coffee left t... team to play in the NFL—and it certainly did ... cause anyone to mention his name among t... pre-season favorites for the Heisman Trophy.

But his progress during spring and summ... practices prompted Saban to start him in t... season-opener against Virginia Tech, and t... bruising tailback responded by rushing for 1... yards and a pair of touchdowns, one on t... ground and the other on a pass reception.

He continued to pile up the yardage and the scores in subsequent games and surged into the Heisman conversation in mid-season when he rushed for a career-high 246 yards against visiting South Carolina, breaking the Bryant-Denny Stadium rushing record. Ingram put an exclamation mark on his 2009 season by rushing for 113 yards and three scores against the Tim Tebow-led and top-ranked Florida Gators in the Southeast Conference championship game. That performance vaulted the Crimson Tide into the No. 1 spot in the national rankings and also assured Ingram a place on the podium as one of the five finalists for the Heisman Trophy. When his name was announced as the 75th winner of the award, Ingram, who

and to give us the best chance to be successful in that game."

Far from letting his team down, Ingram rocked the Longhorns' defense for 116 yards and two scores, helping Alabama to achieve a 37-21 victory and their 13th national title. Coincidentally, the game was played at the Rose Bowl Stadium, in Pasadena, California, where the Tide won their first national championship 84 years earlier, in 1926.

Ingram, however, is not about to rest on his laurels and, instead, he's been preparing as hard as he can to lead the Crimson Tide to a second consecutive B.C.S. title and, while he's at it, to join the former Ohio State running back Archie Griffin as the only other player ever to win a second Heisman Trophy.

The four other finalists for the 2009 Heisman Trophy were Tim Tebow, Colt McCoy, Ndamukong Suh, and Toby Gerhart, the closest-ever second-place finisher.

set a school record with 1,542 yards rushing and scored 15 touchdowns, sobbed as he spoke through his tears of joy.

"It was a real special moment for me that I'll cherish for the rest of my life, and I'm so excited to bring Alabama its first Heisman Trophy winner," said Ingram, who offered thanks to his family, coaches, and teammates, but who then quickly turned his attention away from his individual honor to the team's upcoming B.C.S. championship game against Texas.

"We start practice on Friday. That's going to be my main focus—the national championship game. My team is looking forward to it. I'm looking forward to it. And I'll do whatever I can to not let them down

"There's always room for improvement," noted Ingram. "The day you stop striving to improve is the day you should stop playing. I'm trying to improve every day. I'm trying to help this team win another SEC championship and get another shot at the national championship. I don't have any pressure. I'm just trying to become the best player I can be."

But whatever happens going forward, the Hall of Champions finally has its missing centerpiece.

"The legacy of Alabama football has certainly filled a void," said Nick Saban, speaking of the Heisman Trophy. "There aren't any holes in the trophy case anymore."

SAM BRADFORD

Although some people insist that leadership requires a large amount of sound and fury, Sam Bradford's career is a clear demonstration of the fact that there is an alternative and, perhaps, more respectful way to rally the troops and make a team more cohesive and productive.

"I am a great leader," declared the usually humble Bradford, who has grown weary of the critical carping about his style of leadership. "If you ask any of my teammates who played with me at Oklahoma, they'll tell you that I was one of the leaders on our team. I can be vocal; a lot of people questioned that. But they don't see what I do in the locker room. I am vocal. I'll get after guys when I need to.

Bradford was an all-around athlete, who also starred in baseball and hockey and, of course, in football, where he was a three-year starter at quarterback and an All-State selection as a senior. And he was also a completely well-rounded student, who earned As in the classroom and played cello in the school's orchestra.

"The biggest story about Sam is what a tremendous young man and role model he is," said Bob Wilson, Bradford's high school football coach. "We didn't know that he'd reach the heights that he has on the football field but we knew that he would be successful at whatever it was that he chose to do with his life, because he's such a bright and mature

Coming out of high school, Bradford was ranked as only the 17th-best prep school quarterback in the nation by several rating agencies.

"But, mostly, I like to lead by example. That's something I believe in. If you don't practice what you preach, then no one's going to follow you. I believe I have all the different leadership styles that you need to be a good leader."

Bradford began developing his work ethic and athletic ability while he was growing up in Oklahoma City, where he was encouraged by his parents to never quit and to try his best in every sport or activity that he signed up for. The Putnam City North High School basketball coach, Bill Robertson, who watched Bradford win a starting spot as a sophomore and then go on to become the Panthers' leading scorer and rebounder and earn All-State honors as a senior, quickly noticed those qualities.

kid and because he's such a tremendous competitor. Some people mistake his easy manner for lack of intensity, but Sam has a burning desire to be the best that he can at anything he does, from checkers to football. When the competition gets stiffer, he seems to step up his performance even more."

Despite his fine qualities and All-State selection, Bradford wasn't a five-star college quarterback prospect, like Tim Tebow or Matthew Stafford, and he wasn't at the top of the 2006 recruiting class, either. In fact, even after the University of Oklahoma awarded him a football scholarship, he didn't initially, create a great impression on his new teammates.

"He wasn't too impressive in early

SAM BRADFORD
008 HEISMAN TROPHY WINNER

practices," recalled former OU running ba[ck]
Jacob Gutierrez. "He just wasn't what we we[re]
accustomed to at the time. Jason White ha[d]
set the bar high by winning the 2003 Heisma[n]
Trophy and we had replaced him with Rh[ett]
Bomar, who looked like the next big thin[g].
We were wondering why we recruit[ed]
this kid."

At the outset, Bradford didn't eve[n]
overwhelm the Sooners' staff, and he w[as]
declared a red-shirt, which meant th[at]
he was ineligible to play during his fi[rst]
season. He was, instead, assigned to t[he]
scout team, which practices against t[he]
first team defense and tries to mimic wh[at]
the upcoming opponent is likely to do [in]
the game.

"Our offensive coaches were pret[ty]
skeptical about him," said Sooners' hea[d]
coach Bob Stoops. "They questioned h[is]
demeanor, but I kept watching his throw[s].
He was just firing the balls all over t[he]
place and completing some really toug[h]
throws against our No. 1 defense eve[ry]
single day. What's more, I could see he w[as]
a real competitor. You don't have to be t[he]
loudest guy in the room to be a leader. I w[as]
really impressed."

Bradford impressed everybody th[e]
following season when he won the startin[g]
job and led the Sooners to an opening-gam[e]
79-10 rout over North Texas. It took hi[m]
less than a minute to throw his first collegia[te]
touchdown pass, a 15-yarder to tight en[d]
Jermaine Gresham, and Bradford then went o[n]
to break the school record for passing yarda[ge]
in a half by throwing for 350 yards. His on[ly]
pass of the second half was his 18th straig[ht]
completion, which tied a Sooners' record th[at]
had been set in 2003 by Jason White.

"Once I got in a rhythm, I felt like, 'I know where I'm going, I know where the ball needs to be, so here it comes,'" said Bradford, who wound up passing for 363 yards and three scores. "This, really, is what you dream about, coming out here and playing in front of 85,000 fans and getting a win like that. "There's not going to be many nights like this one. This was special."

In fact, Bradford enjoyed many similar outings as he set the NCAA freshman record for touchdown passes in a season, with 36, and led the nation with a 176.53 passing efficiency rating, finishing just ahead of Florida signal-caller Tim Tebow. Bradford's marksmanship helped to lead the OU to the Big 12 Championship and the No. 4 national

Bradford also led the nation in touchdown passes, with 50, and passing efficiency, and was named the winner of the Heisman Trophy for those incredible numbers and for leading OU to a 12-1 record and its second consecutive Big 12 title.

"Wow, I wasn't expecting this," said Bradford, who was also named the winner of the Davey O'Brien Award for being the best college quarterback in the country and the Sammy Baugh Trophy for being the best collegiate passer. "Earlier today I looked at the portraits of the other Heisman winners on the wall, and it was hard to consider myself on the same level as those guys. But here I am. I know it's an individual award, but I'm receiving it on behalf of my teammates."

"I was really nervous," said Bradford, about his Heisman experience. "I'd rather play in front of 100,000 people than wait for an award to be given."

ranking, despite a loss to West Virginia in the Fiesta Bowl.

"By the time we got to 2007, he was confident and level-headed, and he had control of the huddle," said Gutierrez. "I came to respect the fact that he's able to be laid back, because when things needed to be done, when it was crunch time, he put us on his shoulders and made the throws he needed to. If you ask me, he can make any situation happen."

As good as Bradford's debut season had been, it still didn't prepare anybody for the pinball-like numbers that he posted in 2008, as he shredded the Sooners' record book and directed an offense that became the highest scoring team in major college history.

Bradford's exciting ride to the top of the college football world came to a crashing halt three weeks afterwards, however, when the high-scoring Sooners' offense was stifled by Florida in the BCS title game and the team suffered a 24-14 defeat.

"In the second half, when we needed to make plays, we just couldn't do it," acknowledged Bradford, who threw two touchdown passes and a pair of picks, while being limited to only 256 passing yards.

Although Bradford could have entered the 2009 NFL draft, he decided to return to OU to try to win the national title that the team had just come so close to achieving.

"When we started the 2008 season, winning the national championship was the first

goal we put down as a team, but we came u
short," said Bradford. "I want another chance

As it turned out, however, Bradford never g
that opportunity because a shoulder injury th
he sustained in Oklahoma's first game sideline
him for almost the entire 2009 season.

"It was really hard on me," said Bradfor
"Going through those last couple of months
the season, not being able to be out there, havir
to go to games and watch…I mean, that ju
killed me."

After Bradford had recovered from his surge
he began to prepare for the upcoming NFL dra
with Terry Shea, who has done prep work wi
numerous pro quarterback hopefuls, includir
Matthew Stafford, the first overall selectio
in the 2009 draft. In a very short time Sh
found out that Bradford was a tireless work
and extremely competitive.

"He's a ferocious competitor, but in a qui
way," explained Shea. "I think that's what h
teammates love about him. Whatever happe
in a game, he keeps the same demeanor."

Bradford also wowed the former Dall
Cowboys executive, Gil Brandt, who had drafte
future Hall-of-Famer Troy Aikman.

"He put on the best quarterback workout l
a prospect that I've seen since I watched Tro
put on a show for us in 1989. And he'll be t
face of your organization because he's one quali
individual."

Billy Devaney, general manager of the S
Louis Rams, concurred with Brandt's assessme
and made Bradford the No. 1 overall pick in th
2010 NFL draft.

"He has a strong arm, his accuracy is off th
charts, and he's a strong leader," said Devane
"I happen to think that he's the whole package

TIM TEBOW
2007 HEISMAN TROPHY WINNER

TIM TEBOW

Tim Tebow is certainly the mo[st] celebrated college football play[er] of the decade, if not of all time, an[d] while grand comparisons, especial[ly] across generations, are not necessari[ly] meaningful, many analysts think th[at] he may be the finest offensive play[er] ever at the collegiate level. Despi[te] his accomplishments, however, the[re] is still a wide group of people wh[o] doubt his ability to succeed as an NF[L] quarterback. But among those wh[o] have played and coached with [or] against him, most are assured th[at] he will, without a doubt, ma[ke] his mark in the pro game, just [as] he did at the University of Florid[a].

"The guy completes a very hig[h] percentage of his passes," note[d] Alabama head coach Nick Saban, wh[o] had tried to recruit Tebow to play f[or] the Crimson Tide when the quarterba[ck] was a high school senior. "He's about [as] good a leader as you could ever expe[ct] at the quarterback position. He has a[ll] of the abilities and has made plays [at] the highest level of college footba[ll]. So, how can that not translate into [a] guy who can play in the NFL? I kno[w] there are some people who pick holes [in] everybody. But this kid is, maybe, o[ne] of the best, or *the best*, college footb[all] player that has ever played the game[."]

Tebow started staking his claim [to] gridiron greatness in his junior season [at] Allen D. Nease High School, in Pon[te] Vedra, Florida, when he set a state record [by] passing for 4,286 yards and was named t[he]

Florida Prep Player of the Year. As a senior, in 2005, Tebow passed for 3,302 yards and tossed 31 touchdown passes, while throwing only four interceptions. With the southpaw quarterback at the throttle, Nease posted a 13-2 record and went on to capture the first state title in the school's history.

"He's a leader like no one else I've ever coached," said Craig Howard, who was Tebow's head coach. "He's always about the team, about making the other players better. He has that special ability to encourage people to play better than they've ever played before."

Tebow was named the Florida Player of the Year for the second consecutive season and he was also selected for the Florida High School Athletic Association's All-Century

After Tebow had made his decision, coach Howard delivered a message to Meyer.

"You aren't just getting a quarterback, you are getting a guy who will change your program," explained Howard. "He will change you. He made me a better coach. I became a better coach because I didn't want to let him down."

Tebow began to fulfill Howard's promise and to earn the respect and affection of his Florida teammates before he had thrown his first touchdown pass or ever run the ball into the end zone.

"I love Tebow," said former Gators' receiver Percy Harvin back in 2006. "He's the hardest worker on the team. He's always first in everything and he always does extra.

> "Hard work beats talent when talent doesn't work hard," said Tebow. "I will work hard to fulfill my dream. I'm going to be a starting quarterback in the NFL."

Team, which listed the top 33 players in the state's 100-year history of high school football.

"He was the most dominant high school quarterback I've ever seen," said Craig Howard. "He turned a mediocre team into a powerhouse, and he did it despite so many people doubting him when he was 14 or 15 years old."

Although he had a wide choice of colleges from which to choose, the *Parade* All-American decided to accept a football scholarship to Florida, mainly because the Gators' head coach, Urban Meyer, employed a spread offense, a system that would optimize Tebow's skill-set by giving him the option to run or pass the football on virtually every play.

If you tell him to run 10 sprints, he'll run 12 of them. And he's always encouraging other people to do well, too. Even if he's doing something, he'll study with you any time you ask. He tries to help everybody be good."

Tebow also showed himself to be a voluble leader, one who plays football with a coiled intensity and who leaves everything out on the gridiron.

"I think that I *am* kind of intense on the field," acknowledged Tebow. "That's how I like to play. It's just because I want to do whatever I can to succeed. I want to push myself in whatever I do to be the best. When you're passionate about something, you care about something, you care a lot about it and you want to do whatever you can to push

yourself and to push your teammates to st
to be the best that they can be."

In his freshman season, Tebow pla
behind three-year starter Chris Leak, who
the Gators to a 13-1 record and a 41-14 u
win over top-ranked Ohio State in the E
Championship Game. But Tebow did pla
significant part in the Gators' season by finish
as the team's second–leading rusher. While
threw only 33 passes, he completed 22 of th
five of which went for touchdowns. He
played a solid role in Florida's title-winn
game by running the ball into the end z
for one score and passing for another.

Tebow took over the starting reins in
sophomore year and proceeded to prod
one of the most outstanding seasons in
annals of college football. He gave a sam
of what was to come in the Gators' oper
game, by throwing for 300 yards and th
scores. In week 4 of the season, Tebow broke
school record for rushing yards by a quarterb
in one game, when he ripped the Univer
of Mississippi defense for 166 yards. His m
amazing performance, however, may have cc
against South Carolina, when he ran for
yards and scored a career-high and a scho
record five touchdowns. Tebow also ripped
Gamecocks' defense for 304 passing yards
two more scores.

He finished the 2007 season with 32
passes and also led the team in rushing v
895 yards and 23 scores, the most single-sea
scoring runs by a quarterback in Divisio
history. In fact, the 55 touchdowns that
passed or ran for were more than 87 *teams* at
Football Bowl Subdivision level had mana
to score during their seasons.

That extraordinary level of product
allowed Tebow to capture a slew of ma
college awards, including the Davey O'Br

Award, which is given to the best quarterback in the nation, and to become the first sophomore ever to win the Heisman Trophy.

"I think it's amazing that you're known forever as a Heisman Trophy winner," said Tebow, who set Southeast Conference records for total yards and touchdowns accounted for and also became the first player in NCAA history to rush for at least 20 scores and to throw for at least 20 touchdowns in a single season. "That's very special. It's overwhelming. I'm kind of at a loss for words."

Although Tebow had had a superlative year, the Gators had stumbled to a disappointing 9-4 record, including a 42-35 loss to the University of Michigan in the Capitol One Bowl, and the team took it upon itself to

about to face for the national championship. "You lose, you lose," said Tebow, with a smile. "We still get to play in January and decide something a little bigger. I'll just use it as motivation, just like the Ole Miss game."

Tebow then went out and delivered the goods by leading the Gators to a 24-14 win over the Sooners, as Florida took home its third national title and its second in three seasons.

After another outstanding season in 2009, Tebow closed out his college career by throwing for a career-high 482 yards and three scores, while sparking the Gators to a 51-24 win over Cincinnati in the Cotton Bowl.

"It was exactly how you want to go out with these seniors and these coaches in your final game together," said Tebow, who also

"His body of work rivals that of anybody else ever to play college football," said Jon Gruden. "The guy's a stud. He's going to be an excellent NFL player."

make a much better showing in 2008. After getting off to a good start, however, the Gators were upset, 31-30, by an unranked Ole Miss team.

When Tebow was asked if he wanted to just forget about the loss and put the game behind him, he said no.

"I want it to stay in our hearts and keep hurting," he explained, "because this will motivate me personally and, I think, everybody else, to never let anything like this happen again."

The Gators responded to the loss by winning all of the remaining games on their schedule and the SEC title. And while Tebow was a Heisman finalist, again, the award went to Sam Bradford, the quarterback for Oklahoma University, the team that the Gators were

ran for 51 yards and a touchdown and who compiled 533 total yards, breaking the BCS record that had been set by Vince Young in the 2005 Rose Bowl. "It just doesn't get any better than this."

Despite his splendid accomplishments, many draft gurus derided the Denver Broncos' decision to select Tebow in the first round of the 2010 draft, pointing to his unpolished throwing motion and his unproven ability to throw deep passes, something that he wasn't asked to do much at Florida. But football analyst Jon Gruden, a former Super Bowl-winning coach, doesn't have any doubts about Tebow's future.

"I'd never bet against Tim Tebow," said Gruden. "He's a winner, period."

REGGIE BUSH

Reggie Bush, a three-year star at the University of Southern California, was one of the most electrifying running backs ever to play college football. He was the type of tailback who comes along once or twice in a generation, reminding people of other indelible talents, such as Hall-of-Famers Gayle Sayers and Barry Sanders, the 1988 Heisman Trophy winner, and Marshall Faulk, who set or tied 19 NCAA records.

"If you've got a linebacker covering him, you might as well start singing their fight song," said former Washington State head coach Bill Doba. "Because no linebacker who ever lived is going to

southern California, began displaying hi amazing ability as a nine-year-old, when h scored seven touchdowns and ran for jus under 300 yards in his first Pop Warne league game. Then, in his second game, h showed that there was room for improvemen by scoring eight touchdowns and romping for 544 yards, numbers more suited for video game than an actual gridiron.

"I couldn't believe what I saw," recalled hi stepfather, Lamar Griffin. "It was like he wa playing at a different speed and at a highe level than the other kids."

Bush also made an instant impression, i 1999, when he ripped off a 60-yard run i his first carry for Helix High School, wher

Reggie Bush was the fifth Trojan tailback to win the Heisman and the seventh overall winner from USC, matching the record held by Notre Dame.

chase down that kid."

Like the Road Runner, Bush had the ability to change direction without slowing down and to stop on a dime, reverse his field and leave linebackers grasping at empty space, looking as though they had been trying to tackle a phantom. Once he had broken into the secondary, he made defensive backs look defenseless against his ability to deke one way and then to shift his feet and instantly accelerate the other way.

"He's a special guy," said former USC center Norm Katnik. "He has the ability to make people miss and he can shake off people like no other back I've ever seen."

Bush, who was born and raised in

he starred in a backfield that also include quarterback Alex Smith, who would becom the first overall selection in the 2005 NF draft. As a junior, the quicksilver tailbac scored 34 touchdowns and collected mor than 3,000 total yards, including rushing an receiving yards and punt and kickoff returns Although he was sidelined with an injury fo four games in his senior season, Bush sti managed to tote the pigskin for nearaly 1,70 yards, averaging an amazing 12.1 yards per carry, and tally 27 touchdowns. Bush, wh had posted the fastest time in the hundre meters among all high school football senior also did the punting for the Highlanders an the coaches gave him the freedom to fak the punt and just take off whenever he saw

REGGIE BUSH
HEISMAN TROPHY WINNER 2005

a crack in the defense.

"Reggie would line up back there and ma[...] 22 defenders miss," recalled former US[...] running backs coach Kennedy Pola, who h[...] scouted Bush for the Trojans and who help[...] to recruit him. "That's 11 twice."

Bush's exploits earned him a spot on t[...] 2002 *USA Today* All-USA First Team and [...] was also named a *Parade* All-American and t[...] magazine's choice as the top running ba[...] in the country. And it took him all of o[...] day at USC for his new teammates to s[...] how dynamic a talent he was.

"He's just so much fun to watch," sa[...] former USC All-American defensive e[...] Kenechi Udeze. "I remember his fi[...] day of practice; he must have run [...] circle around the whole defense a[...] then sprinted into the end zone fo[...] touchdown. Of course, it was even more f[...] watching him do it to opposing defenses on[...] the season started."

During Bush's freshman year, head coa[...] Pete Carroll used him in a complementary r[...] on a Trojan team that was stacked with A[...] Americans, including quarterback Matt Leina[...] and which finished the season as the No.[...] ranked squad in the nation in the Associat[...] Press poll. Although he had only 90 carri[...] Bush made the most of them, rushing for 5[...] yards and three scores, and he also took the b[...] into the end zone on four of his 15 receptio[...] as well as on a kickoff return. His 1,330 a[...] purpose yards broke USC's freshman reco[...] and every time he touched the ball he sen[...] jolt of excitement through the stadium an[...] ripple of anxiety through opposing defenses[...]

"When he's on the field, you hear lineback[...] screaming out his number on every pla[...] recalled former teammate Alex Holmes. "Th[...] were all shouting, 'No. 5, No. 5.' Reggie i[...]

guy who literally changes the tenor of the game just by being out there."

Bush's talent and versatility also created nightmare visions for coaches when they tried to game-plan against him and, even more so, when they saw him shredding their defenses in real time.

"On one play he shows that he's as good as any receiver on their team, and the next play he's running with power and making guys miss," noted former BYU head coach Gary Crowton. "And he's so fast that he can go the distance any time he touches the ball. He just has the ability to create lots of match-up problems without them needing to change their personnel groups. That's a real luxury for

himself in the hot seat and laid down a challenge to any and all 2005 Heisman hopefuls.

"I'll be back next year," declared the Trojan tailback, who had finished fifth in the voting, behind Leinart, a pair of Oklahoma Sooners, running back Adrian Peterson and quarterback Jason White, and Utah quarterback Alex Smith—the first time that former high school teammates had ever been Heisman finalists together. "My best football is still ahead of me."

Bush didn't just talk the talk, either, but spent the off-season working out with LaDainian Tomlinson, who was an All-Pro running back with the San Diego Chargers.

Reggie Bush and Matt Leinart are the first set of Heisman Trophy-winning teammates ever to play in a game together.

a coach to have."

Bush continued to sparkle in his sophomore season, as he compiled 2,300 total yards and scored 15 touchdowns, including two on a pair of long-distance punt returns of more than 50 yards each.

"A punt return is almost like freedom of speech," said Bush. "You get to go out and do whatever you want. It's not a set-up play. I just go out there and express my athleticism, my personality, and the type of player that I am."

His contributions not only helped to lift USC to an undefeated season and a BCS Championship Game win over Oklahoma, it also propelled him on to the stage as one of the five finalists for the 2004 Heisman Trophy. Although he didn't win the award—his teammate, Matt Leinart, did—Bush put

Tomlinson, who signed to play with the New York Jets in 2001, was quick to notice a similarity between himself and Bush.

"I noticed some of myself in him, as far as creativity goes," said L.T. "He likes to express himself and do different things with the football. He can line up as receiver and run any pass route, and he can line up in the backfield and take it to you, inside or outside."

The experience of working out with Tomlinson was an eye-opener for Bush, who came to realize that there were still higher levels to reach.

"LaDainian showed me what it takes to be the best running back in the NFL and for me to be the best running back in college football," said Bush. "I went back to USC with a new focus."

Bush proved that he was better than eve[r] 2005 by amassing 2,890 total yards, break[ing] the Pac-10 Conference record, and help[ing] to lead the Trojans to a 12-0 record and t[he] 34th consecutive win.

"He's such a special player, a once-[in]-a-lifetime talent," said Pete Carroll. "H[e's] a game-changer, with his speed, instin[ct,] vision, and competitiveness. He's jus[t so] much fun to watch."

Bush also delivered on his year-[long] promise by winning the 2005 Heism[an] Trophy, beating out Vince Young a[nd] Leinart, who finished third.

"This is amazing," said Bush, w[ho] also won the Doak Walker Award as [the] nation's premiere running back. "I[t] truly is an honor to be elected into the frater[nity] of Heisman winners."

Unfortunately for Bush, Young was abl[e to] get the last laugh when he put on one of [the] greatest performances in college footb[all] history and led Texas to a last-seco[nd] 41-38 triumph over USC in the R[ose] Bowl. The loss ended USC's winn[ing] streak and also allowed Texas to leapf[rog] over the Trojans in the national rankings [and] to capture the BCS title.

Although Bush had ended his coll[ege] career on that disappointing note, his spi[rits] were soon buoyed when the New Orle[ans] Saints selected him with the second overall p[ick] in the 2005 NFL draft. And while Bush ha[s not] enjoyed the same type of success in the NFL t[hat] he had in college, he did play a substantial [role] in helping the Saints to achieve their first-e[ver] Super Bowl win following the 2009 season.

"I've always dreamed about hoisting up [a] Super Bowl trophy," said Bush. "This is what [it's] all about, making dreams come true."

22

CARSON PALMER
2002 HEISMAN TROPHY WINNER

CARSON PALMER

After three seasons as the starting quarterba[ck] for the University of Southern Californ[ia] Carson Palmer's college career seem[ed] destined to end in utter mediocrity. The Troja[ns] had won only half of his 32 starts and his onc[e] bright prospects had been further dimmed [by] his inconsistent play and his tendency to thro[w] interceptions, including a school record-tyi[ng] 18 in his sophomore year.

"The 2000 season was a huge learni[ng] experience," said Palmer. "It made me grow [up] a lot more as a quarterback. I was shocked wh[en] I looked back and saw all those interception[s.] A couple of times I would try to make pla[ys] when there was nothing there and then I'd g[et] frustrated and the next time I'd try even har[der] to force the ball into non-existent opening[s.] It backfired almost every time."

Palmer, who was born and raised [in] southern California, had harbored a dream [of] playing for USC since he was a ninth-grad[er] when a friend's parents would take him to s[ee] the Trojans play.

"I just fell in love with everything about th[eir] football games and their tradition," recall[ed] Palmer. "I always imagined myself running o[ut] of the Coliseum tunnel and onto the field."

Palmer began turning his dream into [a] reality at Santa Margarita High School, whe[re] he quickly established himself as a passer to [be] watched before he had played his first vars[ity] game.

"In high school, the whole varsity wou[ld] watch his freshman games and just stand [in] awe," recalled former USC wide receiv[er] Matt Nickles, who was Palmer's pr[ep] school teammate. "I knew this guy w[as] going to be big-time some day."

As a junior, in 1996, Palmer led Santa Margarita to a 13-1 mark and a division title, while tossing 25 touchdown passes and only five interceptions.

"In high school, you're not prepared for quarterbacks like him," noted DeShaun Foster, a prep school rival of Palmer's, who went on to play tailback for USC's cross-town rival, UCLA. "Carson's arm was unbelievably strong and he was such an accurate passer."

Palmer's stature increased even higher after a senior season in which he threw for 31 scores and was picked only four times, while completing 63 percent of his passes and leading the Eagles to an undefeated season and a second successive divisional championship. Palmer delivered his most outstanding performance in that title game,

Although he didn't have any expectations of starting as a freshman, he was, nonetheless, thrust into that position towards the end of the season, and the fit wasn't really a comfortable one for him.

"Just trying to learn the playbook was so overwhelming," recalled Palmer. "I didn't really know what was going on. Everyone looked like they were moving at a million miles an hour and I was just guessing what I should do on about 20 percent of the plays."

An injury to his throwing shoulder sidelined Palmer for most of the following season but his time away from the game allowed him to see that he wasn't working as hard as he thought he was or needed to if he wanted to achieve the success that he craved.

"It made me realize that I couldn't take

"My heart's about to come out of my shirt," said Palmer, as he accepted the Heisman Trophy. "This has been amazing, this whole journey through this season."

as he threw for a school-record 416 yards and five touchdowns, and rushed for a sixth score.

"Carson has the size of Troy Aikman and the arm strength of John Elway," said Palmer's high school coach, Jim Hartigan, who favorably compared him to three Hall of Fame quarterbacks. "He's got the super-quick release of Dan Marino and the ability to put zip on the ball or touch, depending on what the situation calls for. He is extremely calm and poised and he always makes the right decisions. He thrives on pressure. The bigger the game, the better he performs."

Palmer left Santa Margarita, in 1998, with 23 school records to his credit and a football scholarship to USC in his pocket.

football for granted," explained Palmer. "You really can't take anything for granted. I used to come to practice and go through the motions. I don't do that anymore. I look forward to practice and enjoy every rep, every snap that I get. Sitting on the sidelines made me understand that you have to use every day in practice to get better. When I got hurt, it gave me a new perspective. Now, I take every snap like it's my last."

But all that additional dedication didn't help him to avoid that disastrous 2000 season or a mediocre one in 2001, the first for offensive coordinator Norm Chow, a quarterback guru who had helped to develop a number of top-flight passers, including

Hall-of-Famer Steve Young and Philip River[s], the San Diego Chargers' Pro Bowl signa[l] caller.

"I had never thrown a comeback or a hoo[k] and-go off a five-step drop before," explaine[d] Palmer. "Coach Chow wants to throw it [a] game, but the key is to take what the defen[se] gives you. I had been greedy, trying to thro[w] the long ball when there's a guy five or s[ix] yards in front of me who's open. He tol[d] me I just have to be more patient."

The following year, all of the effor[t] combined with the tutelage of Chow, final[ly] kicked in and Palmer soared to the top [of] the college football world by winning th[e] 2002 Heisman Trophy and the Johnn[y] Unitas Golden Arm Award as the nation[s] top senior quarterback.

"This has been amazing," said Palmer, wh[o] set numerous single-season school record[s] including yards passing and touchdow[n] passes, and who concluded his college care[er] by being named the MVP in the Troja[ns] Orange Bowl win.

"It was really emotional for Carson to wi[n] the Heisman after several years of struggling[,]" said Pete Carroll, who was USC's head coac[h]. "To come out of the ashes and finish on [a] high note was really fun to watch."

Palmer's final season was such a game[-] changer that it convinced the Cincinna[ti] Bengals to make him the No. 1 pick i[n] the 2003 NFL draft and he has gone on t[o] reward their choice by becoming a Pro Bow[l] quarterback and by leading the Bengals to [a] pair of AFC North titles.

"He's a bright guy, who wants to improv[e] and become great," said Ron Jaworski, [a] former Pro Bowl quarterback, who is now [a] football analyst. "He's a winner."

CHARLES WOODSON
1997 HEISMAN TROPHY WINNER

CHARLES WOODSON

Even when he was an untried NF rookie, in 1998, Charles Woodsc displayed a supreme confidence in h ability to succeed against the league's t offensive players.

"I mean, there is a maturity jump," not Woodson, whom the Oakland Raiders h selected with the fourth overall pick of t draft. "You're playing with and against gu who are thirty years old, have kids, and wh are trying to put food on their tables, bu never know any way but to succeed. I did in high school, in college, and now I'll do in the pros."

Woodson started developing his se confidence as a young boy, when he watch his single mother, Georgia, cope wi and then transcend life's difficultie Although she worked at two jobs wh raising her three children by herse she never complained or allowed tho tough circumstances to defeat her. H powerful example allowed her son to devel the assurance that, whatever life might bri his way, he, too, could face up to it and successful.

"That's a gift from my mother," explain Woodson. "Whenever I feel pressure I ca lean on the fact that I've always excelle always been good at what I've done, ev since childhood. That's a really importa feeling to have, especially at my position. you're a cornerback and you look unsure yourself, it will be a long day for you."